Caring for people with learning disabilities who are dying

About the authors

Noelle Blackman, is a State Registered Dramatherapist and founder of the **roc** Loss and Bereavement Service, a unique therapeutic service for people with learning disabilities which also provided training and support to professionals and carers. She is currently the Assistant Director of Respond (a psychotherapy service for people with learning disabilities). Noelle has published and presented many papers on loss, bereavement and dying, both nationally and internationally. Amongst other publications, she is co-author of *"When Somebody Dies"* (Gaskell) and author of *"Loss and Learning Disability"* (Worth Publishing). She is also co-facilitator of the GOLD Group and Vice co-ordinator of the National Network for the Palliative Care for People with Learning Disabilities.

Dr Stuart Todd is a Senior Research Fellow at the Welsh Centre for Learning Disabilities. The Centre is a specialist teaching and research centre within Cardiff University. Over 30 years, the centre has developed a reputation for leading edge research across the life span in areas such as residential services, supported employment, family life, health and identity, complemented by recent research on death, dying and learning disabilities. Stuart is also a member of the National Network for Palliative Care for People with Learning Disabilities and the Death, Dying and Disability group within IASSID, an international body devoted to research within the area of learning disabilities.

Caring for people with learning disabilities who are dying

Noëlle Blackman
(RESPOND, London)

and Stuart Todd
(Welsh Centre for Learning Disabilities,
CARDIFF UNIVERSITY)

Worth Publishing

www.worthpublishing.com

First published 2005 by Worth Publishing Ltd
9 Charlotte Road, London SW13 9QJ
www.worthpublishing.com

Printed and bound in Great Britain by Bath Press, Bath, UK

British Library Cataloguing in Publication Data
A catalogue record for this book is available from the British Library

ISBN 1-903269-17-2

Front cover photograph by Robert Tyler

Cover and text design by Anna Murphy

Acknowledgements

The authors would like to thank the Henry Smith Charity for their support in the making of this book. Death and dying are not topics that many funders wish to have associated with learning disabilities. Without their support, and without the encouragement of Lady Clare Euston, the work that led to this book would not have occurred.

We would also like to thank the following colleagues and friends for their comments and helpful suggestions in the drafting of this book:- Paul Coe, Joan Follett, Darren Lelliot, Edwin Jones, Linda McEnhill, Philips Funeral Directors (St Albans), Claud Regnard, Jackie Saunders, and Karen Wakelin.

To all those who care

In memory of Kevin Gask, who taught all
those who cared for him so much

Contents

Foreword

Linda S McEnhill

Co-ordinator The National Network for the Palliative
Care of People with Learning Disabilities
Associate Hambro-Macmillan Fellow (2003)

I have a colleague who says that some thoughts are so hard to bear, that it's rather like trying to hold very hot plates in your hands. You can only do so for an instant before you simply have to put them down. Death, it appears, is one of this kind of thought. The thought of our own mortality, or worse still, that of someone we care for, is a thought just 'too hot to handle'.

As service providers, however, we have to bear such thoughts. Not only to imagine the death of one of our service users, but to hold the thought long enough to consider all the implications of such a death. This book will enable services to do just that.

Death in a residential setting is akin to a large pebble being dropped into a pool of water. The ripples continue to spread out for a long time afterwards and have impact far further than one could ever have expected. And as in any 'family', the ripples begin to spread through the circles of residents, staff, family and friends right from the moment we learn that death is imminent, long before the actual death.

The authors of this book, Stuart Todd and Noelle Blackman, point out that many services have policies concerning the death of service users, but that these tend, on the whole, to be 'post mortem', in other words, after the event. Dead bodies do tend to galvanise us into action, and quite rightly, agencies have developed policies on management of funerals, the person's estate and some have even considered bereavement care for surviving residents. However, there seems to be a real lack of thinking about how to work with a resident who is dying, as opposed to how to handle their death. *Caring for People with Learning Disabilities Who Are Dying* thus makes a uniquely valuable contribution in aiding services to consider the issues, *"Who should be told about the impending death?"* and *"How should they be told?"*. It considers in depth the practical matters of how to identify and deal with distress, what to expect as the person deteriorates physically, which services to call upon and what you can expect from them. It considers the complex issues involved in working with the client's biological family, recognising their emotional needs, whilst still meeting those of the client's residential 'family'.

It is clear that this guidance is written from Stuart and Noelle's extensive experience of working with service users in these settings. Throughout every section, consideration is given not only to the needs of the dying client, the other service users and the client's family, but also to the needs of you and your colleagues, the staff trying to achieve 'a good death' for your client, often in the most difficult of situations. Thus the suggestions for good practice are couched in concern for your well-being and for your own inevitable mourning process, something which is often neglected under the guise of it 'just being part of the job'.

I know from the weekly phone calls that the Network receives that the advice in this book is both necessary and timely. Its concern for its readers is essential, in enabling a move away from death as a traumatic event towards regarding death as part of the process of one's life, and in some cases even a defining achievement. I strongly recommend this book to you and your colleagues.

Introduction

This book draws upon our personal and professional working experience with people with learning disabilities and their carers. It has been prompted by our discovery that learning disability services are often poorly prepared for dealing with the dying phase of a person's life. We have listened to many stories where people have said, *"We wished it could have been better!"*

When someone is dying, they are likely to have a new set of needs and wishes that may be difficult to talk about. Although the person may be dying, they still have a life and relationships that continue to need fulfilling. However, alongside meeting these wishes, there is a need for some sort of acceptance and preparation for the impending death. The people likely to do most of the work of caring for a person with learning disabilities who is dying will be you, the direct care staff, who may have little expertise or training in being with a person when they are dying.

Other residents' needs can easily become overlooked during the crisis of a terminal illness. We would like to highlight ways in which this risk can be minimised. Sadly, we also feel that staff are often not given sufficient opportunity to talk about their concerns and fears, or to talk over their experiences of caring for someone who has died. Too often, people are left in pain and in silence. Staff have their own needs for support, that can be easily neglected when they are the people who are providing the support to the individual who is dying. Their emotional needs should be responded to *whilst* they are in the midst of caring for someone who is dying, and also after the person's death.

So we have prepared the information in this small book with service managers and support workers in specialist learning disability supported living services in mind. Our aims are:

> to provide a resource and stimulus for discussions on how a service might respond to the needs of an individual with a learning disability who is dying

> to help staff recognise and respond to the needs of others whom the dying and death of that person will affect, including family, friends and other residents

> to enable staff to recognise their own needs for training and support, and to help them identify resources which can meet these needs

This book outlines different aspects of dying and bereavement, to be used as an initial guide to complicated and delicate issues. We hope it will be read *proactively*. It won't provide all the answers to questions staff may have on how to effectively care for someone who is dying - it couldn't! Death and dying are amongst the most profound and complex events of all human experience. Our more modest aim is to provide both a creative starting point for staff working with people with learning disabilities on which to base your own more detailed discussion, and some help in identifying sources of support.

Caring for People with Learning Disablities who are Dying can be used to consider how a service should support people with learning disabilities in the future. Of course there are many services which will have already cared for a person as they died. However, it seems to us that learning which may come out of experiences like this can too easily become lost. Often there is no discussion about how well the service responded to a dying individual, to his or her family and friends, to support staff, or to the other people who may have lived in the same house. As part of preparing your service to deal with dying, this book could also be used to review past experiences, and to develop good practice based on them.

Throughout this book, we urge you and your colleagues to consider not only the needs of the individual who is dying, but the needs of all the people involved in their care and support. Our concern is with encouraging people to be prepared for and to be able to reflect upon and review how a service manages and responds to the challenges of dying. The information in this book cannot meet all these needs, but we hope that it will help you to consider and prepare for some difficult but potentially rewarding challenges. We hope that you, the reader, and your colleagues, will wish to continue to develop your understanding and resourcefulness in your work with people with learning disabilities who are dying. Additional resources and contacts for more detailed help, advice and information can be found at the back of the book.

Chapter 1

"A good death" - can dying ever be good?

When people with learning disabilities move into a residential service, they are usually offered 'a home for life'. This means that as a staff member, you may be involved in someone's care when he or she receives a terminal diagnosis, and from this point right up to their eventual death. When a service has been developed around the principle of supporting people to live life as fully as possible, it can be very hard to switch to supporting those same people through illness towards death. The service will have been very committed to giving people their right to an ordinary life. Now it is challenged by death, and you or other staff members may feel frightened, guilty and uncertain about how to manage what is sometimes termed, a 'good death'. After all, it is likely that neither you nor your colleagues entered this type of work to care for someone who is dying. The ethos of your work and commitment has been a 'good life'. A 'good death' may feel like a contradiction. However, the issue here is not that death is 'good' but *ensuring that life whilst dying is good*: in other words, that choices are still led by the person that you are caring for, and that they are supported to live what is left of their life in as full, satisfying and comfortable a way as possible. The ideas of choice, dignity and respect become more important throughout this time, not less, as do the watchwords 'inclusion' and 'individuality'.

What can we hope for?
A 'good death' is a frequently used phrase. There is a sense that in these days of technology, we can have control over everything, even

death. So use of the phrase may be an attempt to make death a less frightening and more orderly process. This is not an understanding we share. Perhaps the best we can hope for is that death is painless; that the person who is dying is able to make some choices over how their illness is managed and how they spend the last stage of their life.

It is likely that the dying phase will be perplexing and unpredictable at times. Supporting someone who has been diagnosed with a terminal illness through to the point of death can be very daunting. However, physical deterioration usually occurs in predictable, gentle steps, making advanced planning possible, although the timescale and emotions involved are less predictable, making flexibility a necessity. So it is important to realise that with good and precise support, dying can often be more easily managed than might be imagined. The extent to which this can be achieved will depend upon the time and effort put into preparing for an individual's death, and a willingness to work in collaboration with many other people. This last point is crucial. The dying person may well be the centre of your thoughts and actions, but it is likely that you will need to look further afield to obtain the support you, your staff and the dying individual needs. This will require planning and time to build new relationships.

It is thus possible to think of a *good enough death*', an idea that allows for the unexpected and still upholds some important principles and values. There may well be a need to revise plans made earlier in the process, but that need not mean compromising the quality of care or the dignity of the individual. By having too idealized a view of how dying will or "should" occur, you might unintentionally cause unnecessary grief for the individual, and, in the long run, for yourself. Holding to a concept of a 'good enough death' may help.

Becoming a bridge between 'old' and 'new'

When someone enters the dying phase of their life you will have to deal with many other people, some familiar, and some new. Some of these people will have been very important in the person's life and may need or expect help from you to enable them to come to terms with the person's impending death. You will also have to deal with other people who will not have figured much in the person's life, but who will have much to offer, both to the person who is dying, and you. Quite often you will find yourself needing to function as the bridge between the old and the new, and as someone who will have to carry out a range of physical, emotional and spiritual tasks with which you may also be unfamiliar. You may not be trained to deal with these demands. You will find that you have support needs of your own.

Summary

- Dying can be gentle and predictable, although the time-scale of events may well be uncertain. The support needs of the individual will change over time. Thus whatever plans you might make initially, these should always be subject to review and revision. When someone is dying, there will nearly always be changes

- Providing good enough end-of-life care will be demanding. It is likely that you and your staff team do not have all the skills necessary to do this. Consider where you might find more specific training

- Do not forget that you and your team will have support needs of your own

As Miguel de Unamuno y Lugo (1921) is reported to have said,

Science says: "We must live," and seeks the means of prolonging, increasing, facilitating and amplifying life, of making it tolerable and acceptable. Wisdom says: "We must die," and seeks how to make us die well.

On the diagnosis of a terminal illness

When someone you are supporting is diagnosed with a terminal illness, you may feel shocked and upset. You may even feel angry and frightened. The range of emotions that death provokes in us can be bewildering in itself. The person you are caring for may be a person you also care about. You may have known this individual very well, after several years of working and living with them. Yet you might be expected to present a 'professional face' to this news. You might feel that to show how you are really feeling would be considered inappropriate, and that you are 'supposed to' put on a bright and cheerful face. This may run contrary to your feelings for the individual.

Initial responses to a diagnosis
The time after a terminal diagnosis is an emotional period, and experiencing a mixture of emotions should not call into question your professional or caring competencies. By recognising this, you are considering both the individual and yourself. You cannot fail to 'feel' death and the weight of its significance. Not only will you have your own emotions to consider, but also those of the individual, relatives and friends, as well as other members of staff. You may also find that the news is a trigger to remembering other ways in which death and dying have touched your life. All these experiences are understandable, and may have to be dealt with.

A terminal illness is an illness for which there is no cure and from which the person will eventually die at some point, possibly soon.

Chapter 2

It is a time when you may hear the phrase, *"Sorry, there is no more that can be done."* However, it is important to remember that this simply means that there is no more that can be done in terms of trying to find a cure. There is still much that can be done for the person in terms of their physical comfort, and in meeting their health, emotional, social and spiritual needs. Meeting these needs may be very demanding for you and others, and effective team-working, with both familiar and new faces, will become essential. Ensuring a 'good enough' death for the person you are caring for will mean looking to outside agencies to support you in your plans. The issue of receiving support from outside agencies is one we feel is very important, and is further discussed below.

Although you may have initial ideas on how to deal with this phase of an individual's life, dying seldom 'goes according to plan', and there will be a need for regular revision and reflection. Although you may draw up a plan for the individual's care shortly after the diagnosis has been made, the process may well have been hasty, without the benefit of adequate consideration or knowledge. As more information comes to hand, plans can be revised to accommodate these. Being flexible in how you deal with dying is not a sign of weakness, nor does it call into question your ability to respond to the needs of the individual. On the contrary, it is the hallmark of high quality care and commitment.

Once you know the truth

Once the news has sunk in that the person with a learning disability that you are caring for is terminally ill, there may be many feelings that trouble you and your colleagues. Expect there to be a mix of reactions to the news that the individual is dying. Even though you may feel confident to deal with these, other members of your team may not. But indeed you may not feel confident, or you may have a fear of not being able to cope. Death may never have been this close before. You may feel frightened because death and dying are perhaps beyond your personal experience. Furthermore, it is likely that you have not had training in caring for a service user who is dying. Although many services state they have 'death policies', these mainly relate to the events that follow an individual's death. These will not prepare you or others to care for someone who is dying over a prolonged period of time. The lack of knowledge and experience within the staff team will have to be addressed and this again highlights the need to look beyond your immediate context for help and support.

This situation may bring up difficult personal issues for some individuals. This should be acknowledged, and the person may need to be taken out of the frontline of care. (From time to time of course, all members of staff need to be taken out of frontline care for supervision and support, both of which are highly confidential). This is the time to think where you might be able to find advice and support from other agencies. We will discuss who these might be later.

Summary

- A diagnosis of terminal illness can provoke a strong mix of emotions, and there is no right way to feel in response to the news

- If you are to support an individual through the dying phase of their life, it is important that you recognise gaps in your own and other people's knowledge and experience

- As you and others go through this phase, you will pick up knowledge and advice that you should then use to revise any initial plans you have made for the individual's care

- This knowledge and experience should also be reviewed after the death of the individual, in order to build up a service's competence in dealing with the experience of dying

Chapter 3

Disclosure: telling a person with learning disabilities that he or she is dying

"I know that this person is going to die, but does she?"

This may be the most challenging question you will have to face; unfortunately, you may have little confidence in your ability to answer it. You will have been told that the person is likely to die soon. Other members of staff and relatives may also have been told that the person is dying. But does the person also know? Should this person know? This section of the book tries to tease out an approach to these questions, and argues that 'telling' is not a once-and-for-all-event. It is best thought of as a process that unfolds little by little over time, with careful monitoring of the individual's reactions to events as they occur.

Who needs to know?

Staff can often find it difficult to talk to people with learning disabilities about painful emotional issues, for example, when a relative dies. If this is the case, it is likely to be even harder to talk to an individual about their own death. Often such news will be given to staff before it is given to the individual. So you and other members of your staff team may know that the person is dying, and their relatives may know too. However, the individual may not know, and this may be the result of a deliberate decision. This is typically taken as a protective decision, based on a genuine belief that the person could not cope with knowing that they are dying.

It is, however, essential for you and your colleagues to think through the rationale and motivation behind such a decision. The decision may have been made because your staff team might find it hard to break such news, or because none of you feel you could cope with the person's emotional response to such news. This would mean that the decision would have been based on staff need, rather than on the best interests of the person who is ill. If this is so, it will be an option that will have important consequences. It can be very hard emotionally to be with someone that you know is dying when they are talking about their future in a positive way, and about the life they are looking forward to. You will have to hide your own feelings very frequently. It also means that the individual will not be able to make decisions about their future care or about things in their lives they might want to resolve before they die.

You cannot make assumptions about how much or how little an individual knows. For some people, even if the individual is in the same room as the doctor when the news is broken, the information may be given in such a way that the person might not be able to understand it. The individual may not know that they are dying, but they may know important changes are taking place in their life without understanding why. They may have considerable anxiety because they have pains that are not clearing up, or they may feel that their health is getting worse. They may notice that other people in their lives are crying more than they used to, or that people are reacting differently to them.

The individual may begin to ask questions, and the answers to those questions require careful deliberation. There will have to be a discussion about how this will be handled. Although there may have been an initial decision to keep such news away from the individual, in the long run, this may be neither useful nor beneficial to anyone. Make decisions gradually about how to deal with this. In the immediate aftermath of a prognosis, it might well be a wise decision not to give the individual the news immediately. However, such delay will simply be a means of 'buying' a little time. It will give the staff group a short breathing space in which to deal with its own initial responses, then to make decisions about how to respond to the new situation, and finally, to draft a preliminary plan.

At some point, in the majority of cases, it will become important for the individual and those close to her or him to share together an understanding that death is approaching. There will be a need to identify the people best placed to talk about this with the individual, and to decide where and how this will be done.

A lot of information, or a little

Although there is a growing belief that individuals who are dying should be told about their condition, the manner in which it is done still requires much careful consideration and discussion. It is our belief that everyone has the right to have as much or as little information as they want. The task here is to find out how much the individual wants to know. The service must be able to commit sufficient resources and effort to doing this properly. If there is some doubt that resources and time are there, then this should inform your decision. Bad news is best given in small digestible pieces, giving straightforward answers to questions asked.

The information may be let out gradually, bit by bit, over a period of time. The obvious changes in a person's routine may, in fact, make it clear that something new, worrying and serious is happening. The first step is therefore to find out how much the individual knows, whether they are worrying about the changes that are happening, and whether they seem keen to be told more. There then needs to be a decision about how much to tell the individual, when to tell them and who might best be suited to do this. This is a discussion that should be held with service managers, care staff and relatives. However, like many of the decisions that are made about caring for someone who is dying, it need not necessarily be a final decision. The plan may need to be reviewed in the light of events and the changing situation.

Much will depend on the cognitive ability of the individual. Someone you perceive to have a reasonable level of understanding needs to be approached in steps.

"How much does this person already understand?"
The person may be fully aware already. A woman, for example, may realise that her breast lump may mean cancer. Another individual will have realised something serious is happening from the trips to hospital and the tests, but may not understand exactly what. Others will not have realised that anything serious is wrong.

"Does he or she want to know more?"
Quite simply, the individual needs to be asked if they want to know more. Some will be clear that they want all the details, but others will be equally clear that they do not want to know more. There will be others who will be uncertain whether or not they want to know more than they already do.

"I think he doesn't wants to know any more!"
or
"I'm not sure she wants to know more!"
A wish not to know more needs to be respected. It is right, however, to check at regular intervals whether the person still feels the same way. For example, a person may be too frightened to hear more information, but as the fear eases they may want more details. The same is true for those who are uncertain about whether they want to hear more information, but in time they may ask. Allowing an individual control over how they gain their information is part of developing trust and a feeling of safety. The key is to make it clear that you are willing to answer questions as and when they are asked.

"She wants to know it all!"
The team needs to plan how to inform the individual about their condition and, at the same time, to be certain that the individual wants the 'whole truth'. We would suggest that you and your staff decide to give such news in the following stages:

WARN: this makes it clear something serious is going on. For example: *"They found the lump in your breast wasn't normal"*.

PAUSE: this allows you to observe the person's reaction. You will know quite quickly whether the person wants to know a little more information: they will either ask a question or look interested. This will prompt you to continue.

CHECK: ask the person if he or she wants you to explain further.

For some individuals you may only have to use the **WARN • PAUSE • CHECK** sequence once, but others may need to go through this process several times.

Once disclosure has begun
Once you have begun to tell the person that their illness is terminal, it is necessary to maintain as consistent an environment as possible for him or her, and to ensure that there is always someone at hand who knows the person well and whom they can trust. We would urge that if and when someone begins to have a full picture of their situation, it is imperative that sufficient support is put in place for the individual to talk openly about their feelings about death and dying, and that there are also plenty of opportunities to ask questions. An individual should not be told of their status and then left alone by staff, who might believe they have 'done their bit'. The individual now knows the truth, but as time passes, they will

need staff to help them cope with the information and its impact on all aspects of their life.

This is an emotionally demanding role. Thought should be given as to how you and other staff will be supported in undertaking it. If there is some uncertainty about the ability to take on this role, it is best to consider whether an outside agency might be able to offer additional support.

Signs of distress

After breaking the bad news, it is crucial to monitor the person for signs of distress and anxiety. These are most likely to be picked up by someone who knows the person well. They will probably become apparent through a change of mood or behaviour, a change in food intake or sleep pattern, or by a difference in the way the person holds themselves or makes eye contact. These might be noted in addition to or instead of more obvious signs, such as tearfulness. It is important to talk with the person about their illness at an appropriate level and pace. Be guided by the person's questions. These will give you an indication of what they feel ready to know and also what they are already beginning to understand.

For an individual with a more severe learning disability, the stages are the same, except that the information will need to be offered in a more accessible form (such as through pictures). The person is likely to require several opportunities to go through the **WARN • PAUSE • CHECK** sequence over several days or weeks. Fear of the unknown may be greater, and so some information may have to be repeated on several occasions.

Even though you may think that the person does not know about their condition, they may show you through the way they behave or the things they say that they actually know more than you have realised. They may show that they are anxious, and may even suspect that their illness is serious and possibly terminal. The person may begin to ask you direct or indirect questions about their health, they might ask questions about their future, or their behaviour might change. He or she may become withdrawn. They may not wish to be on their own. At this stage you and your colleagues will need to consider how such questions will be answered, and how you are going to respond to an individual's hidden concerns. Agreement between staff and relatives should be reached so as to provide a consistent approach.

Working at the person's own pace

It may be that the individual has been told that they are dying, but they seem to be carrying on as if they had not been told. That is, they know, but appear to be pretending not to know. This is a very delicate situation for you to deal with. The individual may be finding it difficult to believe that he or she is dying and may need more time. It is essential not to rush someone struggling in this way. Not believing that death will really happen may be a very useful coping mechanism for some people, and should be respected as such.

Other people may benefit from an opportunity to talk, and want to share their feelings. This may be very difficult for you emotionally. The person may need to talk about their feelings, they may want to know more about what the news may mean for their immediate future. They may ask questions such as – *"Will it hurt?"*, *"What is it like to die?"*, *"Who will remember me?"* They might want to think with you about making a will. All these are difficult issues to think about and respond to, and you may need some support to work out how to deal with them. A bereavement counsellor or the local palliative care team should be able to support you. We recommend that you do not hesitate to approach these services, and ask for their support.

You have a very important part to play in supporting this individual in a variety of ways, including giving him or her time and opportunity to talk about death and about their wishes. It can be both an onerous and rewarding task to support someone in this way. This is why it is so important to share this with others, and look for support throughout this process.

Summary

- Telling a person with a learning disability that he or she is dying may be best thought of as a process that may take weeks, months or even longer to go through, rather than as an event to be 'done' only once

- How much or how little the person is told will depend on their wishes and understanding. Disclosure should always happen at the person's own pace

- You have a very important part to play in supporting this individual, and for giving the person time and opportunity for talking about death, their feelings and wishes

- This can be a rewarding but demanding task, so seeking support from outside agencies is strongly recommended

Chapter 4

Working with dying and death - planning and partnerships

For many years, you may have been coming to a place of work where the focus has been helping people live as full a life as possible. Over time, you will have come to be comfortable and confident in this. You will have learned how best to support people in a mixture of different ways: alongside other staff, from experience or through training.

Now, however, your place of work has changed. It is now a place where you are supporting someone who is dying. And you may not have the experience and training to do this. The other people you work with may be in a similar situation. There are other people involved in this person's life who may also need support, for example, friends and family. The time to look for a way to support all these people, including the individual and yourself, is NOW.

Developing a network

It is important to put plans in place to support the individual when a terminal illness is diagnosed. At the beginning, the person may not even seem ill, and is still capable of participating in ordinary day-to-day activities and special events. Even where this is the case, it is still important to plan ahead and to think about the needs of others, and where advice and support can be obtained about preparing for the next stages of the person's life. The longer you delay or put off thinking about potential support needs and resources, the less time you will have to get them established, and the less effective they will be.

The period following diagnosis is the time to consider, *"Who is around?"*, *"What help do we need?"*, *"Who might be able to help us?"* and also, *"Who might need more support?"* Indeed, we would argue that many services should think about how they might prepare for caring for people at the end of their lives before service users enter the dying phase. Resources and supports can then be built up in advance. Training can be provided before it is required. Making contact with local hospices, palliative care services or bereavement counsellors before someone needs them may seem morbid. But it may well help you and your colleagues deliver effective and confident support should the need for it ever arise.

When an individual is diagnosed with a terminal illness, you may find yourself having to deal with professionals and services with whom you have not had much contact in the past. At the outset these new relationships may feel awkward. There may be a certain amount of rivalry or you might find that there are strains and tensions in some of these relationships which will need to be resolved. Indeed you may anticipate that there will be such tensions and, therefore, avoid making contact with other professional groups. For example, you may feel, *"They don't know anything about people with learning disabilities They will only make things worse!"*

These groups actually may not have much experience of people with learning disabilities. It will be your role and responsibility to help them understand and learn, always remembering that the important person in the middle of all of this is the person you are supporting. It becomes essential to find ways of rising above any minor conflicts, in order to serve the person with learning disabilities to the best of your abilities. It is important to remember that you and your colleagues will always have an important role to play, regardless of the other professionals and agencies that become involved in the individual's care. The wealth of knowledge that the residential staff have should always be shared with relatives and other professionals. This knowledge may make all the difference in providing effective care of a high quality. Ideally, therefore, care should be provided in partnership with all involved, with a sharing of skills and knowledge between both learning disability and palliative care services.

Families

We hope that you and your service have already built up strong and positive working partnerships with the families of the users of your service. However, these relationships may not be as positive as you might wish. The relationship between services and families can be fraught. Yet, whether these relationships are good, bad or indifferent, feelings and sensitivities may run high at the point of a terminal diagnosis. The family may wish to take a more active role than they have had in the past. They may even wish for their relative to return to the family home. Or it may be that they feel the individual would be best cared for in another setting. It is also possible that the family may wish to be less involved than they have been before. It can be very hard for the staff group to accept situations in which the family appears to be asking for more control over events. The staff group may well feel that they have been the person's 'family' for some time. Relatives may feel that they are being kept at a distance. These tensions are likely to be present in many cases, to some extent.

Staff should be made aware that there are many good reasons why the individual initially left the family home. It is part-and-parcel of family life for its members to move on. Yet people in services can sometimes feel that the family gave up the right to care for the individual when they entered the service. This is often not true at all. As for all of us, we can be at the very heart of our own families without having to live with them or be surrounded by them. When family members know that one of their own is dying, they may seek different relationships with the individual than those they had in the past. They may be motivated by a sense of duty or tradition. The change might be attributable to an opportunity to make peace. There could be many reasons for the way families deal with news that a relative is dying, but it is unhelpful for staff to 'second guess' what those reasons are. Relatives' feelings should be respected as their way of showing concern for a loved member of their family. One way to circumvent any potential tension is to bring the family into discussions about the care of their relative as early as possible. This needs to be done in a way that makes clear that key decisions have not yet been made.

Getting together

It is probably best that the service initiates contact with families, by asking them to come and discuss the next steps in the provision of care for the person. Any plans the service has tentatively made should be put forward as provisional plans for discussion, and not as decisions for comment. You and your colleagues should talk confidently and openly about how you can continue to provide care for the individual, and offer information about the network of support available. You, or your service, may not, for example, have had any experience in caring for people who are dying. If this is the case, you should suggest where you might get support from and ask the family for their ideas and contributions. Even if you have had such experience, you must also recognize that for many families there will be important traditions or customs that they would like to have taken into account. The family have a right to have their views listened to and respected, and they also need a chance to hear your views and those of your service.

Most families want to feel secure that their relative will be well looked after, and that their own concerns will be heard. Many families will be also be looking to offer and receive support. They should also be supported to prepare themselves for the pain of loss and separation. Allow the family to be a part of the emotional world that surrounds dying. It is important to respect the views and feelings of families, and to support them wherever possible. Their needs may be considerable. The service might be able to offer this support simply through the attitude it adopts towards the family. Additionally, there may be other services and professionals who you will come into contact with over the dying phase who may also be in a position to provide emotional and spiritual support to the family, and thus share the work with you.

The GP

When someone has a terminal illness, they will either have or will soon develop health needs that require support from outside the residential service. These needs and changes should be discussed with the person's GP as soon as possible. It is important to remember that the GP may not know all the services available. It can therefore be very useful to talk to a GP with a prepared set of questions about the person's condition, and about possible services which might help. Some of these are listed below, and there are further resources at the end of the book. If these services are not offered voluntarily by a GP then ask for them, if you think they might be useful.

District nurses, Macmillan nurses and Marie Curie nurses

★ A District nurse should be involved as soon as possible after a diagnosis of terminal illness is made, as they can be a gateway to many other services. Contact with a District nurse can be obtained through your GP. It is likely that it will be difficult for you to recognise the changing health care needs of the person, or indeed know how to respond to them. The District nurse can assess when and whether further help is needed

★ Macmillan nurses are palliative care specialists who provide expert information, advice and emotional support to people living with cancer, their families, friends and carers, throughout the UK. Some health teams have a palliative care consultant who can provide additional specialist advice. They have received specialist training in managing pain and other symptoms, and in psychological support. They are, therefore, people who will be familiar with many of the problems with which you are now dealing, perhaps for the first time

★ Marie Curie nurses will provide direct or hands-on nursing care for the individual, including moving and handling. This type of support can be invaluable, especially if the service did not have to provide such support to the individual when they were well. They can provide both practical and emotional advice and support to the patient and carers. They will monitor the person's condition and inform District nurses about changes to assist in planning future care. They have up-to-date experience of working in hospitals or the community

There may well be nurses who provide such care for people who are dying from illnesses other than cancer. We would recommend that you talk to local or national agencies about this.

Other professionals

It may be important to involve other professionals such as: a dietician, a physiotherapist, a speech therapist, a dental service, twighlight nurses, counselling services or Arts therapists. These professionals can have much to offer the individual, the family and the staff group. It would be impossible to do justice to the contribution these professionals can make in this short book. For the moment, we feel that is worth raising the possibility of their involvement as a question to be addressed by the team, nurse or GP; *"Does this person need... ?"*

Palliative care

There is a belief that palliative care means hospice care. This is not so. Palliative care is an umbrella term for a very wide range of possible services. The World Health Organisation defines palliative care as -

> ...the active total care of patients whose disease is not responsive to curative treatment. Control of pain, of other symptoms, and of psychological, social and spiritual problems, is paramount. The goal of palliative care is achievement of the best quality of life for patients and their families.   (WHO 2002)

Palliative care is necessarily multidisciplinary. You can expect that palliative care professionals will listen to you as well as the patient, since their interest and expertise extend beyond the medical and nursing needs of the individual to include the needs of the wider system surrounding the patient. This means that they are likely to also offer advice on dealing with not only the emotional needs of the individual but the emotional needs of relatives, staff and other residents. If for some reason they do not, you are entitled to ask for this. These are, after all, professionals, whose daily business is facing the perplexities and issues that dying provokes.

Specialist palliative care teams contain a range of professionals, which can include nurses, doctors, physiotherapists, occupational therapists, social workers, psychologists, counsellors and spiritual care co-ordinators. Such teams can therefore offer a range of support in a variety of settings. However, it is also important to remember that they may not know much about the needs of people with learning disabilities. This is why, at several points in this booklet, we have stressed making contact with these professionals as early as possible. You may feel that the person does not have palliative care needs at this stage. However, they will or may well do soon. Contact with palliative care services should be made as soon as possible so that everyone has an opportunity to plan and prepare for the time when those needs become real. It is to the benefit of everyone involved that this done early rather than when an illness becomes more severe and life limiting. Early contact will give the palliative care professionals the opportunity to acquaint themselves with the specific needs of the person with learning disabilities before the illness takes hold. You and your colleagues will have an essential part to play in this process.

When you come into contact with the world of palliative care, you may do so with some reservations or uncertainties about these services. You might have preconceived ideas that it is 'just' another medical service, or one that does not value life. However, the philosophy behind the modern palliative care system overlaps in many ways with the philosophy that underpins the modern learning disability service system. You will find a service system that:

- affirms life and regards dying as a normal process
- neither hastens nor postpones death
- provides relief from pain and other distressing symptoms
- integrates the psychological and spiritual aspects of care
- offers a support system to help patients live as actively as possible until death
- offers a support system to help patients' families and other supportive networks cope during the patient's illness and in their own bereavement

(developed from the WHO definition of palliative care)

When palliative care services become involved, this does not mean that the learning disability service has surrendered its care for the individual. It also does not mean that the service has failed the individual. If the person's needs change so much that they have to be admitted into hospice care, the learning disability service still has much to offer in terms of the individual's emotional and physical support needs. In *Loss and Learning Disability*, (Blackman 2003 pages 31-33) a case example is given of a young man with severe learning disabilities who was terminally ill in hospital. His time there was greatly enhanced by the residential staff from his home, who made sure that his environment was conducive to him feeling good about himself. The staff who knew him well furnished his hospital room with sensory objects and other things which were familiar to him, in order to help him to feel more relaxed. His needs in this context were an education to the hospital staff.

We noted above that palliative care professionals will have seen the many different sides of dying. They may not have had much experience in caring for someone with learning disabilities. The people who know the individual well will be you and your colleagues from learning disability services. Caring for someone who is dying is a complex and demanding task. No one individual has the necessary skills to deal with it by him or herself, or to be able to make all the right decisions. If inter-disciplinary work is important in learning disability services, it is essential in the care of the dying.

Spiritual/religious support

The spiritual and religious needs of the individual should be seen and treated as important. Some individuals may have ongoing contact with religious communities or networks that might also be a part of the supportive network for the dying individual. Even if individuals have not had recent contact with such groups or contact with them in the time they have been living in the service setting, they may now find that they have religious needs which have been dormant up until this point. The service should be willing to admit that such information may have been lost, and that families might still consider their spiritual beliefs important in the life of their relative. Cultural customs should also be considered at this point. Some people may wish to see a spiritual leader as death approaches. Others, for example, may need to be supported to be lying in a certain way when the final days approach – facing Mecca, for example, or being moved from a bed onto the floor.

Spiritual support does not always mean input from formal religion. For some people, spirituality is represented by concerns, wondering, and asking questions about the great and the small things about living. Such questing draws us into conversation with other people, where we can talk with openness about our lives and ourselves. It is a way of expressing our feelings about being in the world. At this time in their lives, people may have many questions that come from wishing to make sense not only of their lives, but also their deaths. Quite simply, people may wish to talk and ask questions about death. Alternatively, it may be that people are not so much searching for meaning but searching to share, to find intimacy. Such conversations do not require you or your colleagues to give or find answers. You may need to do no more than sit and listen, or to touch, or hold someone's hand. The conversation might mean exchanging views and fears. Whatever is required will take time, and it may take training. As we have stated elsewhere, to be done well, it will also require support.

Drawing up a plan for care through the dying stage

At diagnosis or shortly afterwards when relevant agencies have been identified, a plan of care should be drawn up. This should be a chance to discuss everyone's wishes and to help everyone involved to set a plan of action and through this to know what they are working towards. Discussions about where the person would like to be cared for, as they become more unwell, should be included here, along with the feelings that the family and the staff from the residential service have about this and any advice or support from the GP, District Nurse and palliative services.

  The key people involved in the planning should be the person themselves (wherever possible), the family (again where possible) and staff (this means palliative care, medical, nursing and learning disability staff). This is the best way to avoid 'crisis decisions' taking place at the last minute. It is also the best way to ensure that changes in the individual's circumstances can be responded to promptly. However, plans cannot be and should not be set in stone. They must be regularly reassessed to check that they are still relevant and appropriate for everyone concerned.

The original plan should then become part of the person's Health Action Plan. It should be written up in their Health Action Plan folder, and be taken with the person on every visit to a health professional. (Health Action Plans are a recommendation made in the English white paper, *Valuing People*, 2001). There may be similar health plans for individuals in other parts of the UK or in other countries. It is important that some record is kept so that information, and notes on wishes and needs can be kept and used by other professionals if necessary. This becomes especially important if the individual has to move from the place they have been living.

Dying, partnerships and planning

The information provided above can be summarised by two key words: partnership and planning. Plans should be sketched out as early as possible, with the proviso that as death approaches and other professionals become involved in the individual's care, these initial plans may well need to be modified. It is crucial that a partnership is maintained between the individual, the family and all the services. It may be difficult for the person with the learning disability to remember and to communicate all the information themselves. In addition, the individual may not have any or full knowledge about their condition. Everyone will hold a different part of the picture.

The family and care staff are likely to have the primary relationships with the person. As part of this group, you help form the bridge between the person with learning disabilities and the medical team, and together you will also notice any small changes in the person. The Macmillan nurse and other palliative care professionals will hold the knowledge about the disease, the treatment, pain relief and access to a range of other services. Regular meetings should be held between all the various parties in order to create a full picture. Decisions should be based on this information, together with the person's wishes. At these meetings, the initial plans for the care of the dying person should be reviewed and revised if necessary.

We cannot stress strongly enough how important we feel it is to work in collaboration with other people, and for you to share your knowledge and expertise with other members of the care team so that a more comprehensive package of care can be delivered. It is part of your duty of care and commitment to listen to and incorporate the views of others. It is also important that these significant people listen to you and your knowledge of the individual.

Summary

- You have been helping people with learning disabilities to live a full life; now you will need to adapt to help them live fully whilst dying

- Partnerships and planning are key to good care for people with learning disabilities who are diagnosed with a terminal illness

- You and your colleagues have a great deal to contribute to the creation and development of effective partnerships with a wide variety of family members, health care and palliative care professionals

- Plans will need to be regularly reviewed as the person's needs and circumstances change, in collaboration with everyone involved

Chapter 5

As death draws closer

For many people nowadays, a fear of dying has replaced the fears our ancestors had of death. Whereas our ancestors were concerned about what happened to their souls after they died, in more recent times our concerns are with the way in which death may occur. For example, we fear painful, lonely and/or distressing deaths. You may have the same fears for the person with learning disabilities who is dying. At this time, you will be having to support the individual through their anxieties, and dealing with your own anxiety and that of your staff. This can be challenging. It will require plenty of support for everyone.

Identifying distress

Many individuals with learning disabilities will be able to communicate that they are distressed, and what is causing their distress. However, some individuals will always have had severe communication difficulties, while others will have developed this difficulty because of their illness (for example, dementia related to Downs syndrome). Distress can show itself by changes in eye contact, facial expressions, skin colour, vocalisations, posture, muscle tone, sleep patterns, appetite, or behaviour. Distress will make some individuals more active, while others may become withdrawn and quiet. Carers often realise something is different but are unsure why; their instinct is often correct. Carers who see the individual intermittently may pick up changes that daily carers have missed. In addition, different carers pick up different signs and behaviours of distress.

Once distress is observed it is important to assess the cause. This can be straightforward. Distress may only occur when a leg is moved, for example, suggesting that this is where the problem lies. Other signs or indications may need input from the district nurse, GP or palliative care specialist. These professionals may suggest possible reasons for distress which can be expected in certain situations (e.g. colic caused by constipation due to analgesics). Noticing distress and identifying the underlying cause is therefore a team activity.

As the person approaches the end of their life, if they have chosen to stay at home, services such as Marie Curie or Twilight nurses can be brought in to deliver nursing care. If, however, you and your service feel unable to cope, it is important that you seek further help. This might mean transferring the person to a hospice or a hospital, especially if there are complex problems that need specialist help. There should be no guilt attached to this decision, and it is still important for you to take an active part in the person's care. If the person is transferred, it is important that you continue to act as a 'bridge' for them, maintaining your relationship and offering your unique knowledge about the person's needs. There are many reasons why a transfer of care will be necessary; the support needs of both the individual and the staff group, and the needs of other residents, should never be under-stated. You and your colleagues should acknowledge to yourselves that you managed to care for the individual in his or her own home for as long as was possible.

Pain control and management of other symptoms

The District nurse, in conjunction with the GP and Macmillan nurse, assesses and delivers pain control. They will need to work in partnership with you to assess the level of discomfort and distress the person is experiencing. They will also assess and manage other symptoms such as – nausea, breathlessness, appetite changes, and fatigue, and offer advice on bowel management and nutrition. They will also be able to offer information and advice on daily activity and on coping strategies including emotional support and living with the changes that the disease may bring about. When pain and other symptoms are managed early on, it is much easier to keep the symptoms under control as the individual becomes more ill. It is a common fear that problems such as pain and breathless get worse as death approaches. This is frequently not the case. Most patients remain settled and comfortable and some problems actually become easier. For example, pain or breathlessness that are worsened by activity will become much less of a problem as an individual becomes chair-bound or bed-bound. Occasionally patients can become unsettled or troubled with respiratory secretions at the end of life. Palliative care services are trained to manage such problems, which is why making contact early is so helpful.

Dying at home

Many people in our society may much prefer to die at home in a familiar setting, and in the company of familiar faces. In reality, this is not what will happen for everyone who wishes it, for a variety of reasons. Another setting might be more useful, or even essential for observation and treatment. Furthermore, during such visits to other settings, the individual's health may unexpectedly deteriorate and make a return home impossible. If the individual has to move from their home or even dies in a place other than home, you should not feel that you have failed this individual. Rather than expect that the individual will die at home, it might be more useful to translate this to read that the majority of the dying phase should happen in the person's own home.

Dying itself is often simple and gentle, but occasionally problems arise that will require specialist help, or sometimes aspects of the disease are difficult for the individual, relatives and carers, such as confusion. So this might mean that from time to time, whilst continuing to live in their familiar environment, the individual will have to access specialist palliative care settings for treatment, or indeed as the disease progresses, the individual might require specialist intervention for the relief of distressing symptoms.

However, many problems can be managed in the home with specialist help. For example, as death approaches, the need for food and water reduces, and specialist advice can help in identifying when there is no longer any need to keep up previous levels of intake. You should ask for and listen to the advice of professionals who have experience in caring for the dying, and knowledge about how dying impacts upon the needs and functioning of the body.

The final phase

You might be worrying about how the person will die; whether they will die alone or whether someone will be with them. This can often create a dilemma. People may struggle with their own fears of being with someone when they die, but at the same time, worry about the person dying alone. You may also not be sure whether the person would want someone with them or not. If someone is very conscious of their impending death, you may be able to have a conversation with them about this. Alternatively, you may be able to discuss it with their family who may choose to be involved.

You will often be able to tell through the person's behaviour. For example, the person may become very anxious when left alone or at night time, which is likely to indicate they would like company. It is an important issue for the staff team to discuss. Discussion may help clarify what you think the person would want if they were able to tell you. You can then decide as a team how you will manage the practicalities of the decision made.

If individuals state quite categorically that they wish to be with the person at the end of their lives, it is important that they are informed of any changes that occur in the person's condition. It is helpful for them to know that unpleasant surprises are very unlikely in the last hours and days. Most patients wind down gently, often slipping in and out of consciousness. Eventually, most people will stay in a coma, their breathing pattern will change, slowing down and eventually stopping. Observers often see it as a gentle absence of life, rather than a sudden presence of death. You might feel that you would be worrying the people who wish to be present unnecessarily, if you were to tell them that the individual has 'taken a turn for the worse', but have no indication whether the person will die soon or not. It is important to remember that you will only be relaying information for others to act on if they so choose. As for 'needlessly worrying' people, these individuals are already worried and concerned, and they will only thank you for keeping them informed.

All of the above is just as important for people who might die in settings outside their own home. As an aspect of an individual's care in a hospice or hospital, make clear arrangements for passing on information about changes in the individual's health.

However, it cannot be guaranteed that the person will be surrounded by familiar people when the end comes. Despite the gentleness of the final hours, the exact time of death is difficult to predict, so death can occur unexpectedly or when people have slipped out of the room. Even if you are not there at the end, it will be important to remember that for the majority of the time whilst the person was dying, people were there when needed.

Summary

- If the person who is dying remains at home, you and your colleagues will be able to observe any pain or distress they are experiencing, and find appropriate care from other agencies to address the underlying cause. This is an important multidisciplinary activity

- Care staff can continue to offer valuable support even if the person needs to move to another setting

- There needs to be discussion as to who should be with the person as death approaches. These people need to be kept informed about changes

Chapter 6

After death: arranging funerals and bereavement support

Our experience tell us that few residential services have procedures and policies about how best to care for a person who is dying. They do, however, often have policies about what to do after an individual has died. Your service may have policies about 'last rites' and these should be checked and reviewed well in advance. However, they may not contain as much information as you need. Your service's policy can be discussed and reviewed along the lines of the information provided below.

"How will I know if the person is dead?"

There are some practical indicators to check if you think that someone has died. There are obvious signs to check for: pulse, pallor, dilated (enlarged) pupils, and so on. Some people describe the body as looking different once the person has died; more relaxed, or sometimes the features looking a little more pointed.

It is important to notify the most senior member of staff as soon as you suspect that the person has died. They will then call a GP to certify the death and to advise on the next step. This will have been discussed beforehand with the GP if it was an expected death and the doctor will often wait until the morning to come out. It is also imperative to break the news to the family (next of kin) straightaway. Action to take after death should be clearly set out well in advance. This should include not only who to inform, but also how to deal with the individual's body. To help you make such decisions within your agency some important information is provided below.

The GP

If the person had not seen their GP (or any other senior doctor) during the previous two weeks, the death would be counted as a sudden death, and the body may have to be left in place while the police or a representative from the coroner's office attend to rule out foul play. If the person had seen the GP recently and the death was expected, this will not be necessary. However, your organisation may have its own policy on this.

GPs will not always come out of hours; it is sometimes possible for a trained medical member of staff or an attendant nurse to declare life extinct. This should be discussed with the GP ahead of the expected death. The GP will then issue a death certificate in the morning.

Care of the body

The care you have shown the individual in life means that you will want to treat the body with respect. Depending on where the person has died, you may want to consider moving the body to a more private place. It is important for you to know that if the body is moved, there may be some leakage of bodily fluids, and also that noises may occur from the lungs as the air is released.

You will need to have checked whether there are any particular cultural or spiritual customs or procedures connected to dying and death which this person would have wanted you to have followed. In some cultures, it would not be appropriate for you to touch the body; for example, within some belief systems, the body of the deceased must only be touched by close relatives.

The heating in the room should be turned off and the room should be slightly ventilated. If possible the body should be straightened and lightly covered. Wherever possible, have a colleague with you while you are with the body. This will help in that there will be someone with whom to share a difficult experience, but just as importantly, it will help to ensure your own security and also that of the service that you work for. As we have already described above, a family's feelings can run high when somebody is dying from a terminal illness, and anger about the death can sometimes become misplaced towards staff in the form of accusations and blame. Therefore, if any jewellery or personal effects are removed (it is a good idea to remove rings before rigor mortis sets in, for example), it is sensible for two people to be present. One person can then remove the items, while the other catalogues them; both people can sign this list. These items should then be locked away for safe-keeping.

You may or may not want to take part in the final ritual of washing and laying out the body. This should be a personal choice. The family should also be offered this choice. If this is something that you would like to do but you feel you need support, you may be able to ask a more experienced member of staff or perhaps a family member to help you, or you may be able to assist the undertaker. However, if you choose, these final rituals may be performed by the undertaker.

Careful consideration should be given to offering people an opportunity to view the body. Family members should be offered this option as should other residents and staff. Seeing that the person has died can be particularly helpful for the other residents with learning disabilities in helping them to understand what has happened. Be open with them and do not try to hide your feelings (as these may help the person to understand their own feelings), or, indeed, the body, if they are showing an interest. Individual's questions and curiosity should give you a guide as to what they are ready for, but it is always a good idea to prepare someone well if they are to view the body, as it can often be distressing.

Removal of the body

Once the death certificate has been issued, the undertaker can be called. An undertaker will often be able to come within the hour, or you may wish to delay their arrival while you take some time to do some of the things discussed above. Either way, you can discuss this with the undertaker. You will hopefully already have ascertained the person's preference for burial or cremation.

You and your service will need to consider how the body is removed from the house, in other words, through which door, and who will be present and who will not. It can be helpful for the other residents to know that the individual's body will be taken away. They may also need to know where it has gone and perhaps something about what will happen to it. Good funeral directors will always try to be discreet and take care of the individual's body. The removal of a body by funeral directors may sometimes be unpleasant to witness. The body will be put into a body bag. If there is a lift that needs to be used, and it is only small, the body will be carried in an upright position. Although rare, this can all be very upsetting. It may be best to make arrangements for this to happen in as discreet a manner as possible, and then to offer to take anyone who feels the need to visit the body at the chapel of rest at a later time.

Summary

- Take time to review your service's policy for after-death care and procedures well in advance of an anticipated death

- Careful consideration should be given to supporting people who wish to be involved in caring for or viewing the body of the deceased

Chapter 7

Saying goodbye

It is important for all staff and residents to be offered the opportunity and appropriate support to attend the funeral. Hopefully the family will be happy for this, although it does of course also depend whether the funeral is held locally or not. Wherever possible, it is helpful to involve other residents in an active way in preparing for the funeral.

Such preparation might include:
- choosing flowers
- choosing what the person wears or what goes in the coffin with them
- saying something at the funeral
- preparing food for the wake, and so on

This of course all needs to be done in partnership with the family. Once again, if working arrangements with families are made at an early stage, hopefully these decisions can be worked out with mutual respect. However, ultimately the family will have a key role to play and although their decisions may run contrary to those of the staff group, they should also be respected. If the family would prefer a quiet and private funeral, then arrangements can be made for staff and residents to mark the individual's death in some other way. This might mean arranging a memorial service locally, or planting a rose bush or tree together (see the section on *Remembering* below).

Supporting staff
Demands on staff are enormous at the time of a resident's death. You will have been stretched and challenged during the period of

the illness. People may have worked over their shift times; the rotas have probably been disturbed. People will be feeling tired both physically and emotionally. There may be uncomfortable feelings of anger, blame or guilt around. On top of all of this, you still need to support other residents and possibly the family of the deceased. It is important for staff to be given the opportunity to discuss their feelings about what has happened, and perhaps to reflect on what went well and what did not, in order to learn how to cope better the next time (although naturally there will be more time for this later). Staff may also need some emotional support either as a group or individually from an external counsellor. If the individual was receiving support from a specialist palliative care service, they may be able to offer this service, or failing that, a local bereavement counselling service such as Cruse *(see Resources p.50)*.

It is important to recognise that experiencing the death of someone you support at work can also trigger feelings connected to other losses in your life. This is not unusual, and it is important to look after yourself and to seek out help.

Supporting other residents

The surviving residents may also benefit from some external emotional support. The palliative care service may offer this. Alternatively, you could contact the local community team for people with learning disabilities to request support from an Arts therapist or a counsellor, or you could contact the local bereavement service, for example, Cruse. (If they have not worked with people with learning disabilities before, you could suggest that they contact the community team in order to learn any extra skills that they might need). These other residents may need emotional support in place before the person dies. They will have experienced the heightened emotions of the staff, and met unfamiliar visitors to the home, some of whom may also be anxious. You may have told them directly what is happening, or they may have guessed. The disclosure process should be similar to that described above for the person who is dying. In other words, it should be led by each individual's wish to know, and should be given bit by bit at a pace that is appropriate for that particular person. It is all too easy for these resident's needs to become overlooked in the rush to meet all the needs of the dying individual.

After the death, the residents will need plenty of support from you. They may want to talk about the person who has died, they may want to visit their room, look at photos of the person or ask endless questions. These are all normal things to be doing, and if you can take time to respond and give them honest answers and time to reminisce, it will be enormously helpful in enabling them to grieve healthily. However, remember that people can express their grief in a variety of ways, and in ways which may not seem typical. As well as having strong feelings about losing the person who has died, for some this death may have awoken unresolved feelings from other losses in their lives, losses, for example, of parents, other family members, children who were taken away, or indeed other residents or staff who have moved on.

People may become distraught; their distress may be expressed verbally or through their behaviour. You may notice people becoming clingier than usual, or you may notice tempers flaring more easily. You may even notice people's sleep patterns or appetites changing. Any changes should be noted in light of the recent bereavement, and opportunities should be given for people to share how they are feeling and to remember time spent with the person who died. If you feel that this is not enough for any individual, it may be that this recent loss has a more deep-rooted connection to other losses, and specialist bereavement counselling should be sought.

Some of the residents may have become worried about their own health and mortality, and may need reassurance. Some people may seem completely unaffected, and can even seem callous; for example, asking if they can have the deceased's room, possessions and so on. This may be because the finality of what has happened has not yet sunk in. But equally, it may also be because people with learning disabilities experience an enormous amount of people coming into and going out of their lives, and there may be some who have learned to cope by not allowing themselves to develop too strong an attachment in the first place. This can be very difficult for staff and other residents who may feel very distressed or even angered by this apparent lack of empathy. Such behaviour may, however, be a prompt for a service to review the life experiences and personal relationships of such people. Together you consider ways of supporting them to cope with the losses that may have already taken place in their lives, and encourage and assist them to develop more personal relationships.

Supporting relatives

Some sensible and sensitive time after an individual's death, your service should consider contacting the relatives of the individuals to ask how they are. This should be seen as a common matter of respect. However, you may also like to ask the family to comment upon how the dying phase was managed and what lessons could be learned for the future. Both queries would be seen as a positive signal about the caring commitment of the service, and as a recognition of the family's loss. All too often, families say that once their relative with a learning disability had died, the service world forgets them. It would be comforting for many families to know they had not been forgotten.

Remembrance and remembering

There is a very modern belief that there is a set period of time for mourning. Some hold the view, for example, that a few days after a funeral we should leave our mourning behind and continue with our lives again, or that we should be 'over it all' completely within a few months. This sort of thinking also holds the belief that the person who has died has no relevance in our daily concerns. However, many people do not feel this way, and beliefs like these can make coping with life very hard for grieving people. The person may have died but they are not lost from memory.

It is useful to find ways to allow those who are grieving a chance to be able to express their continuing bond. It is important to provide opportunities which enable the other residents to remember and reminisce about the person who has died, in a manner which feels natural and comfortable. This will help many in their grieving, but will also help them to see that they too will be remembered when they themselves die.

In the days following the death, it will be important for the remaining residents to see that the room of the person who has died is now empty. This will be a very real way for them to begin to realise that the person is no longer there. It may also provoke questions, which may provide a helpful beginning in allowing individuals to realise the full extent of what has happened. If the family members of the deceased are willing, it may also be helpful for the residents to be given the opportunity to choose a small memento from the deceased's room as a token of remembrance.

Some services create a 'wall of memories' (McEnhill 1999). This consists of one of the walls in the building being used to display photos of people who have moved from the service, who no longer work there, or who have died. This can become a 'concrete' visual focal point for residents and staff to enjoying talking about those people who are no longer in the house. It is also a good idea to have photo albums and videos with images of the person who has died kept in an accessible place, so that the residents can choose to look at them and reminisce alone or with a member of staff or another resident.

Residents should be given the opportunity to visit the grave or garden of remembrance after the funeral, and as often as they would like to after this. It is also important to respect the decision of those who do not wish to do this.

Death is not a fleeting stranger in learning disability services. Many people will have lived and died in the services that exist now for people with a learning disability. Perhaps individual services or even a collection of services might dedicate a day as a day of remembrance, where relatives, staff (past and present) and friends could come together to meet and share memories. This need not be a solemn day or involve religious activities. It could be simply a gathering to remember lives that were valued by others. In so doing, value is added to our own lives.

Summary

- Attending the funeral of the person who has died is just one of the ways to remember the person and to help you and your colleagues, residents and family members grieve

- Residents may display their grief in a variety of ways, and may well need support

- Finding ways to remember the person gives a positive message to residents that they too are and will always be valued

- Initiating contact with relatives of the person who has died indicates commitment to them and to the person who has died

- Learning from the process of supporting the person until their death can be integrated into future policy and practice

Chapter 8

Final thoughts

We feel it might be helpful for you to compare your sense of confidence and feelings about supporting someone through a dying phase now, with those you may have had before reading this book. Your commitment to providing good and compassionate care will not have changed. We believe that the overwhelming majority of people who provide support to people with learning disabilities do so from a sense of dedication and a shared sense of humanity.

Our own experience has told us that when someone is dying, support staff want to provide good quality end-of-life care as a mark of dignity and respect. It is also the hallmark of a good human service. How we treat people at the end of their life says much about the type of people we are. However, we have seen people become frustrated at the lack of support they receive to do this. Too much can be expected of people. We have also seen what happens when people have a simplistic or over idealized view of what dying can entail. It is a complex process, at physical, spiritual and emotional levels.

We hope that we have shown that this complexity can be lessened by building up working partnerships with professionals from palliative care services. Your commitment to provide compassionate care will still be high. We hope we have added to that in showing how you can be both supportive and supported in seeing this commitment reach its best expression: a good enough death!

Providing end-of-life care proves that your work and the work of your colleagues is more than just a job. You are willing to face the challenges of life and death. We hope we have given you some indication of what these challenges may be, some confidence to face these challenges and some insight into the support you and the person you are caring for deserve.

Resources

WEBSITES AND ORGANISATIONS

The National Network for the Palliative Care of People with Learning Disabilities (NNPCPLD)

The NNPCPLD was set up in November 1998. It was established by a small group of practitioners from both learning disability and palliative care services who were concerned that people with learning disabilities were not routinely accessing palliative care services when confronted with life threatening/limiting illnesses.

Website under development:

www.helpthehospices.org.uk/professional/dsp_professional.asp

Contact Co-ordinator: Linda McEnhill

linda.mcenhill@st-nicholas-hospice.org.uk

Downs Syndrome Association	www.downs-syndrome.org.uk
Foundation for People with Learning Disabilities	www.learningdisabilities.org.uk
Help the Hospices	www.helpthehospices.org.uk
Macmillan Cancer Relief	www.macmillan.org.uk
Marie Curie Cancer Care	www.mariecurie.org.uk
Mencap	www.mencap.org.uk
National Association Of Funeral Directors	www.nafd.org.uk
The National Council for Palliative Care	www.ncpc.org.uk
World Health Organisation	www.who/int/en/

VIDEOS

Speak Up Self Advocacy (1997) *Coping with Death* Speak Up Self Advocacy,
   43 Holm Flatt Street, Parkgate, Rotherham, South Yorkshire, S62 6HJ.
   Tel 01709 710199
* A video made by and for people with learning disabilities, explaining what
   happens when someone dies

BEREAVEMENT SERVICES

Most community learning disability teams should be able offer bereavement
counselling from the psychologists, Arts therapy practitioners and/or counsellors
or psychotherapists who make up their team

Cruse Bereavement Care, Cruse House, 126 Sheen Road, Surrey TW9 1UR.
   Tel: 020 8939 9530. Day by Day is the Cruse National Helpline 0870 167
   1677. Cruse offers general bereavement counselling. Telephone Cruse House
   for details of your local Cruse branch.

RESPOND offers a therapy service to people with learning disabilities in London
   Euston and surrounding area. RESPOND also offers training and support to
   carers throughout the UK. Tel: 020 7383 0700 Fax: 020 7387 1222
   www.respond.org.uk
   RESPOND also has a national telephone helpline service 0808 808 0700

References

GENERAL BACKGROUND READING

Blackman, N. (2004) *Loss and Learning Disability*
  London: Worth Publishing

Brown, H., Burns, S., Flynn, M. (in press) *Dying Matters: A Training Pack for Staff
  in Learning Disability and Palliative Care Services* UK: Foundation for People with
  Learning Disabilities

Cobb, M. (2001) *The Dying Soul: Spiritual Care at the End of Life*
  Buckingham, UK: Open University Press

Jones, A. & Tuffrey-Winje, I. (2002) *Positive Approaches to Palliative Care Workbook*
  Kidderminster, UK: BILD Publications

Katz, J. & Peace, S. (2003) *End of Life in Care Homes*
  Oxford, UK: Oxford University Press

Lindop, P. & Read, S. (2000) District nurses' needs: palliative care for people with
  learning disabilities *International Journal of Palliative Nursing*, 6, 117-22

McEnhill, L. (2004) Disability in Olivere, B and Monroe, B (Eds) *Death, Dying and
  Social Difference* Oxford, UK: Oxford University Press

McEnhill, L. S. (1999) Guided mourning interventions, in *Living with Loss: Helping
  People with Learning Disabilities Cope with Bereavement and Loss* Blackman, N. (Ed.)
  Brighton UK: Pavilion Publishing

McNamara, B. (2001) *Fragile Lives: Death, Dying and Care*
  Buckingham, UK: Open University Press

National Council for Hospice and Specialist Palliative Care Services (2001) What
  do we mean by palliative care? a discussion paper. *Briefing no. 9.*
  London: NCHDPCS Northgate Palliative Care Team DISTAT Northgate and
  Prudhoe Trust

Read, S. (Ed.) 2004. *Palliative Care for People with Learning Disabilities*
  London: Quay Books

Regnard, C., Matthews, D., Gibson, L., Clarke, C., & Watson, B., Difficulties in
    identifying distress and its causes in people with severe communication
    problems International Journal of Palliative Nursing, 2003, 9(3): 173-6

Regnard, C., Gibson, L. & Jenson, R. (2004) CLiP (Current Learning in Palliative
    Care) Helping the Person with Advanced Disease: a Workbook.
    Oxford: Radcliffe Medical Press

Todd, S. (2002) Death does not become us Journal of Gerontological Social Work,
    38, 225-240

Todd, S. (2004) A Troubled History: Death and learning disability.
    In S. Read (Ed). Palliative Care for People with Learning Disabilities.
    London: Quay Books

Tuffrey-Wijne, I. (1997) Palliative care and learning disabilities.
    Nursing Times: 93(31): 50-51.

Tuffrey-Wijne, I. (2003) Getting on with Cancer (Learning Disabilities).
    London: Royal College of Psychiatry

Tuffrey-Wijne, I. (2003) The palliative care needs of people with interllectual
    disablities: a literature review Palliative Medicine 17: 55-62

Unamuno, M. de (1976)(Tr. Spanish, Flitch, J.E.C) Tragic Sense of Life
    NY, USA: Dover Publishing

TITLES ON BEREAVEMENT

Books Beyond Words (St. George's Hospital Medical School, London SW17)
This series tell stories on important and often difficult themes, including
death and bereavement, through pictures
Hollins, S. & Sireling, L. (1989) *When Dad Died* London: St George's Mental
Health Library
Hollins, S. & Sireling, L. (1989) *When Mum Died* London: St George's Mental
Health Library
Hollins, S., Dowling, S. & Blackman, N. (2003) *When Somebody Dies* London:
Gaskell

Cathcart, F. (1994) *Understanding Death and Dying (Series)* Worcestershire: British
Institute of Learning Disabilities
Cooley, J. & McGauran, F. (2000) *Talking Together About Death - A bereavement
pack for people with learning disabilities, their families and carers*
Bicester, UK: Speechmark Publishing
Heegaard, M. (1988) *When Someone Very Special Dies* USA: Woodland Press
Holland, A., Payne, A. & Vickery, L (1998) *Exploring Your Emotions* Worcestershire,
UK: British Institute of Learning Disabilities.
Hollins, S. & Sireling, L (1991) *Understanding Grief: Working with Grief and People
who have Learning Disabilities* Brighton UK: Pavilion Publishing
Luchterhand, C. & Murphy, N. (1998) *Helping Adults with Mental Retardation
Grieve a Death Loss* Accelerated Development: (USA): Taylor and Francis (UK)
Nottingham Healthcare NHS Trust Learning Disability Directorate (1999)
Bereavement Guidelines
Persaud, S. & Persaud, M. (2003) *Loss and Bereavement for People with
Learning Disabilities* Derbyshire NHS Mental Health Services NHS Trust.
Buckinghamshire, UK: Wordsmith Publications
Stuart, M. (1997) *Looking Back, Looking Forward: Reminiscence with People with
Learning Difficulties* Brighton, UK: Pavilion Publishing
• A bereavement information pack which aims to provide carers of
people with learning disabilities with some practical indicators enabling
them to support people who have experienced loss and bereavement.
Resource containing pictures, signs and symbols